LEVEL
1

Animal Homes

Shira Evans

NATIONAL GEOGRAPHIC

Washington, D.C.

Animals need a place to live.

Some animals make their homes.

honeybees

Bees make a hive.

Birds use grass and twigs.

masked weaver

They make a nest.

Some bats sleep in caves.
They hang on to the rocks.

Some homes are low down.

A fox lives in a den. It's in the ground.

Foxes often make their dens near the base of a tree.

bald eagle

Some homes are high up.

A bird lives in a nest.
It's up in a tree.

Some animals sleep in many places. Deer walk all day.

Then they find
a new place to rest.

grizzly bears

Other animals sleep in one home all the time.

Some bears sleep in a den.
They sleep there all winter.

Some homes are for one animal.

orb-weaver spider

A spider lives on a web.
It lives alone.

Other homes are for
animal families.

Rabbits live together.
They live in a burrow.

There are many kinds of homes.
Some homes even move!

hermit crab

YOUR TURN!

Match each animal to its home.

1. spider

a. hive

2. rabbits

b. nest

3. bee

c. burrow

4. bird

d. web

For Sam and Alex. —S.E.

The author and publisher gratefully acknowledge the expert content review of this book by Jason Matthews, master naturalist, Montana Natural History Center/Montana Outdoor Science School, and the literacy review of this book by Kimberly Gillow, principal, Milan Area Schools, Michigan.

This British English edition published in 2020 by Collins, an imprint of HarperCollins*Publishers*
The News Building, 1 London Bridge Street, London. SE1 9GF.

Browse the complete Collins catalogue at
www.collins.co.uk

British Library Cataloguing-in-Publication Data
A catalogue record for this publication is available from the British Library.

NATIONAL GEOGRAPHIC and Yellow Border Design are trademarks of the National Geographic Society, used under license.

Designed by Sanjida Rashid

ISBN: 978-0-00-842223-3
US edition ISBN: 978-1-4263-3026-1
On the cover: A Cape ground squirrel peeks out from its burrow.
Photo Credits
Cover, Jean-Jacques Alcalay/Minden Pictures; 1, Michael
Siluk/UIG/Getty Images; 2-3, Sean Russell/Getty Images; 4, nayneung1/Getty Images; 5, brandtbolding/Getty Images; 6-7, Shumba138/Getty Images; 8, Gunter Ziesler/Getty Images; 9, Alasdair Turner/Getty Images; 10-11, Steve Oehlenschlager/Getty Images; 12-13 (BACKGROUND), Michael S. Quinton/National Geographic Creative; 13 (INSET), Jean-edouard Rozey/Dreamstime; 14, Martin Mecnarowski/Shutterstock; 15, epantha/Getty Images; 16-17, blickwinkel/Alamy Stock Photo; 18-19, papkin/Shutterstock; 20-21, stanley45/Getty Images; 22, Serge_Vero/Getty Images; 23 (1), sarintra chimphoolsuk/Shutterstock; 23 (2), William Booth/Shutterstock; 23 (3), sumikophoto/Shutterstock; 23 (4), Alex Snyder; 23 (A), stockphoto mania/Shutterstock; 23 (B), Claudia Paulussen/Dreamstime; 23 (C), MartialRed/Getty Images; 23 (D), Hellen Grig/Shutterstock; 24, Jack Nevitt/Shutterstock

Printed and bound in India by Replika Press Pvt. Ltd.